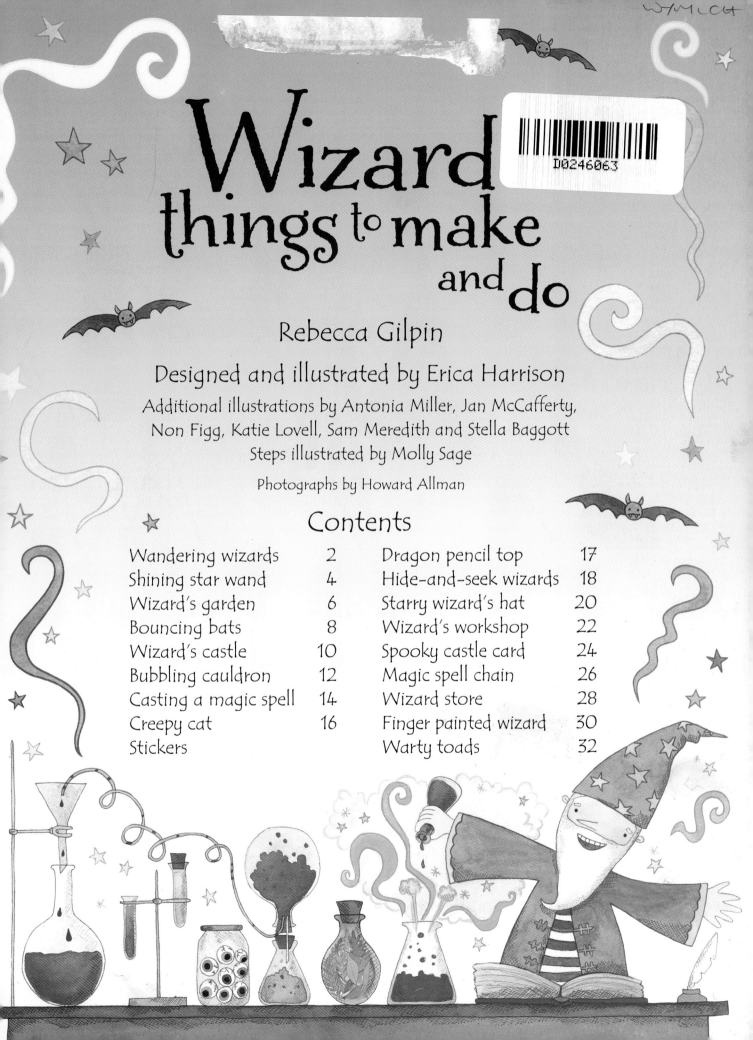

Wizard things to make and do

Rebecca Gilpin

Designed and illustrated by Erica Harrison

Additional illustrations by Antonia Miller, Jan McCafferty,
Non Figg, Katie Lovell, Sam Meredith and Stella Baggott
Steps illustrated by Molly Sage

Photographs by Howard Allman

Contents

Wandering wizards

1. To make a cone for the wizard, lay a plate on a piece of paper and draw around it. Then, cut out the circle and cut it in half.

2. Put one half to the side. Then, bend the other half over, until the points meet. Pinch the paper in the middle to make a mark.

Look at this picture for ideas for decorating your wizard.

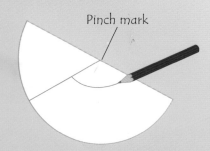

Pinch mark

3. Draw a line from the pinch mark to the curved edge, about a third of the way around. Then, draw a curve for the wizard's hat.

4. Draw a shape for the wizard's head below the middle of his hat. Draw ears, a beard and hair, then draw his face.

To make a wand, press two star stickers onto the end of a strip of thick paper.

Use a gold or silver pen, if you have one.

5. Draw two arms on the other half circle, then cut them out. Decorate the wizard with felt-tip pens, then erase any pencil lines.

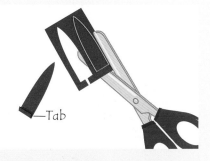

Line up the edge with the pencil line.

6. Spread glue on the plain paper next to the pencil line. Then, bend the paper around to make a cone and press the edges together.

—Tab

7. For the feet, draw two pointed shapes on bright paper. Cut them out, then fold over the square end of each one, to make a tab.

Only glue the tops of the arms.

8. Tape the tabs on the feet onto the inside of the body. Curl the pointed ends with your fingers. Then, glue on the arms.

Shining star wand

Make the slots the same length.

1. Glue shiny paper on both sides of thin cardboard. Draw a star, then cut it out. Lay it on the cardboard, then draw around it again.

2. Draw a mark at the top of the first star, then move it off the cardboard. Draw a mark at the top of the second star, then cut it out.

3. Keeping the marks at the top, cut a slot into each star, like this. Make the slots the same thickness as the cardboard.

4. Hold the stars so that the slots line up, like this. Then, gently push them together, to make the top of the wand.

Roll the paper at a slight angle.

5. Tightly roll a large piece of paper for the stick, then tape the edge to secure it. Trim a little piece off each end to make them neat.

4

Slot one star into each slot.

6. Make four cuts into the top of the stick, spacing them evenly. Slot the stars into the cuts, then tape the stick onto the stars.

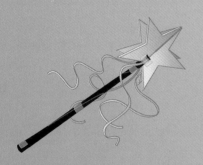

The stars on this wand were decorated with shiny stickers from this book.

7. Cut four pieces of gift ribbon, making them a little shorter than the wand. Tape the pieces of ribbon between the stars, like this.

This will make eight stars.

8. For the little stars, fold a strip of shiny paper in half. Draw four stars on the paper, then cut them out, holding the layers together.

9. Glue one of the stars onto the end of a ribbon, then press another star on top. Glue on the other stars in the same way.

For a striped wand, wrap gift ribbon around the wand and tape it to secure it.

5

Wizard's garden

Cut a little way outside the lines.

Draw the wizard's face with a thin black pen.

Fingers

1. Draw a robe on a piece of paper and cut it out. Draw around it on another piece of paper, then add an apron. Cut out the apron.

2. Glue the robe onto a big piece of paper, then glue on the apron. Cut out shapes for the wizard's face, beard and hat, then glue them on.

3. Cut out two hands and glue them on. Cut out a watering can and glue it on, too. Then, glue an oval over the handle, for fingers.

Look at this picture for ideas of things to have in your wizard's garden.

You could add a pocket on the apron with a fork and trowel in it.

4. Draw big curling plants on pieces of bright paper. Cut them out, then glue them around the wizard, leaving gaps between them.

5. For fly-eating plants, draw an '8' shape on green paper and a smaller one on pink paper. Cut them out and glue them on, like this.

Add a stalk, too.

6. Draw over all the pencil lines with a thin black pen. Add lines and spots on the plants. Then, draw stars on the wizard's apron.

Use a silver pen, if you have one.

Add a castle-shaped bat table, with bats flying around it.

Bouncing bats

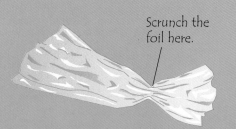

Scrunch the foil here.

1. Cut a rectangle of kitchen foil for the bat's body. Then, scrunch it tightly, about a third of the way along, like this.

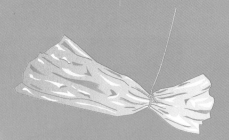

2. Cut a long, thin rubber band, to make a long piece for hanging the bat. Tie one end tightly around the scrunched part of the foil.

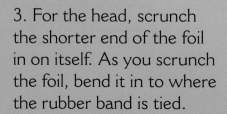

3. For the head, scrunch the shorter end of the foil in on itself. As you scrunch the foil, bend it in to where the rubber band is tied.

Make sure that the rubber band still sticks out of the middle.

4. Scrunch the other end of the foil in the same way, to make the body. Then, squeeze the head and body, to make them rounded.

Pull the rubber band out to one side.

5. Rip lots of small pieces of black tissue paper. Then, lay the bat on plastic foodwrap and brush part of it with white glue.

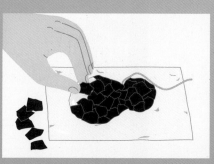

6. Press pieces of tissue paper onto the wet glue. Then, brush on more glue and press on more paper, until the bat is covered.

Fold —

Hold the layers together as you cut.

7. Fold a strip of black paper in half, with the short ends together. Draw a wing shape against the fold, then cut out the shape.

Fold the tabs up, like this.

8. Draw two ears on black paper, with a tab at the bottom. Cut out the ears, then glue their tabs, and the wings, onto the bat.

Hang up the bat while the glue dries.

9. Draw the bat's mouth with a silver pen. Then, draw eyes and fangs on white paper. Cut them out, then glue them on.

9

Wizard's castle

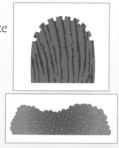

The entrance needs to be narrower than the trees.

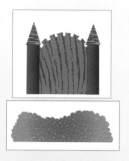

Make sure that the entrance is still narrower than the trees.

Make the bottom edge straight.

1. Rip patterned pieces of paper from old magazines. On one, draw a long shape for bushes. Cut it out and glue it onto thin cardboard.

2. For the castle's entrance, draw a rounded shape, then cut it out. Cut tiny squares from the top, then glue the shape onto thin cardboard.

3. Cut out two rectangles for towers. Glue them on, overlapping the entrance a little. Then, glue on two triangles for roofs.

You could glue leaf shapes onto the bushes at the bottom.

4. Cut an arch for a doorway and glue it onto the entrance. Then, cut a smaller shape for a door and glue it on top, like this.

5. Cut a square for the top of the castle, making it narrower than the entrance. Cut tiny squares from the top. Then, cut a roof, too.

Make more layers for a tall, thin castle.

The towers need to overlap the square.

6. Glue the roof, then the square, onto another piece of thin cardboard. Cut a thin strip of paper and two towers, then glue them on.

Tape the bushes at the bottom.

7. Cut out the three pictures, leaving a thin white border around the edges. Then, tape them together on the back.

8. Draw windows with a black felt-tip pen and press on stickers from this book. Then, gently bend the castle so that it stands up.

Bubbling cauldron

Draw an oval for the open top of the cauldron.

1. Using a pencil, draw a cauldron at the bottom of a large piece of paper. Then, add swirling steam and bubbles with a green pencil.

The crayon is shown here in yellow so that you can see it.

Fill in the bubbles, too.

2. Pressing hard with a white wax crayon, draw over the green swirls. Add shapes inside the bubbles, then draw more swirls.

3. Brush water all over the paper, then blob on watery green paint. Brush darker paint over the swirls, then leave it to dry completely.

This picture had pink paint added in step 3.

Look at the big picture for ideas of what to draw.

4. Paint the cauldron with thick black paint. Then, while the paint dries, draw ingredients for a spell on another piece of paper.

5. Fill in the pictures with chalk pastels, wax crayons or pencils, then cut them out. Then, cut out pictures from old magazines, too.

6. Glue some pictures in the cauldron and others around it. Then, press on star stickers and glue on shiny paper shapes.

Casting a magic spell

1. Using a pencil, draw a curved line for the wizard's nose, near the top of a piece of white paper. Then, add two dots for his eyes.

2. Starting at the top of the nose, draw a pointed hat. Add the wizard's whiskers and beard, then draw his hair.

3. Draw a big triangle with a curve at the bottom for the wizard's robe. Then, add two lines in the middle of the robe for his gown.

4. Draw two long triangles for flowing sleeves. Then, add the hands, with a line coming from one of them, for his wand.

5. Using watery paints, paint the wizard's face, hands, hair, whiskers and beard. Then, paint his robe and gown, too.

6. Leave the paint to dry completely. Then, carefully draw over all the pencil lines with a thin black felt-tip pen.

7. Using gold glitter glue, draw lines along the edges of his robe, sleeves and the bottom of the hat. Then, add lots of spots, too.

8. Draw gold and purple glitter glue swirls coming from the wand. Smudge some of the swirls a little, with the tip of your finger.

9. While the glitter glue is still wet, press on star sequins. Press one onto the end of his wand, then glue some onto his gown, too.

Creepy cat

You could add spikes for fur, too.

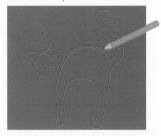

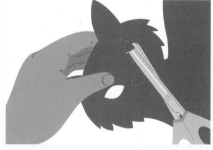

1. Draw an arched body and legs on orange paper. Add a head, face and tail, then erase the lines where they meet the body.

2. Carefully cut out the cat. Then, pinch the paper in the middle of one eye. Using scissors, make a cut in the middle, like this.

3. Push one blade of the scissors into the cut, then carefully cut around the cat's eye. Cut out the other eye and the nose, too.

If you tape your cat to a window, light shines through the eyes and nose.

You could make a black cat, too.

Draw the pupils on the front of the eyes.

4. Cut two pieces of green tissue paper, a little bigger than the eyes. Tape one to the back of each eye, then draw a pupil on each one.

5. Tape a piece of pink tissue paper to the back of the cat's nose. Then, use pencils to draw markings on the cat, like this.

Dragon pencil top

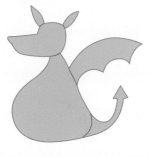

1. Draw a dragon's head on a piece of paper. Add a rounded body, a wing and a tail. Cut out the dragon, then erase the pencil lines.

2. Lay the dragon back on the paper and carefully draw around it. Then, cut around the second dragon, along the outline.

The dragon shapes need to face each other.

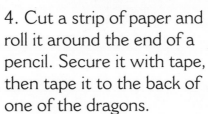

3. Outline the dragons with a black felt-tip pen. Draw their arms and legs. Add a face on one of them, then add spots with a pencil, too.

4. Cut a strip of paper and roll it around the end of a pencil. Secure it with tape, then tape it to the back of one of the dragons.

Bend the wings out a little.

5. Spread glue all over the dragon, except for its wings. Press the other dragon on top and hold them until the glue sticks.

Hide-and-seek wizards

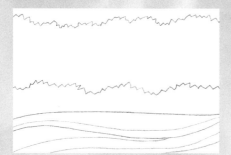

Leave spaces between the trees.

1. Draw several long wavy lines across the bottom of a piece of white paper, for grass. Add two long zigzag lines above them for leaves.

2. For each tree, draw two lines for the trunk. Then, join the trunk to the leaves with lots of branches and twigs, like this.

3. Draw lots more trees, then erase the grass where it overlaps the trees. Add lots of lines for bark on the trunks, too.

You could draw wizards hiding behind bushes, too.

Try drawing wizards hiding in the tops of the trees.

Add wizards flying in the sky on broomsticks.

4. Next to a tree, draw a wizard's head, pointed hat and robes. Erase any grass that he overlaps, then add his sleeve, hand and face.

5. Draw more wizards playing hide-and-seek behind the trees. Then, draw over all the outlines with a black ballpoint pen.

6. Draw lots and lots of vertical lines between the trees, for shadows. Then, fill in the wizards, trees and sky with runny paints.

You could add wizards hiding in the roots of a tree.

Starry wizard's hat

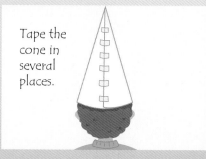

Tape the cone in several places.

Don't worry if the circles aren't exactly round.

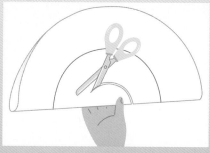

1. Cut a half circle from a large piece of thick paper. Get someone to bend it into a cone around your head, then tape it together.

2. To make the brim, put the cone on another piece of paper. Draw around the cone. Then, draw a bigger circle around the outside.

3. Cut out the big circle. Bend it in half and hold it in the middle. Then, carefully cut a small half circle out of the middle.

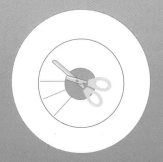

4. Flatten the paper again. Then, make about 10 cuts from the small circle out to the pencil line, but don't cut over the line.

Tape the flaps like this.

5. Lay the brim on top of the open end of the cone. Then, bend each flap down and tape it inside the cone, to secure the brim.

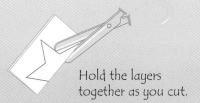

Hold the layers together as you cut.

6. To decorate the hat, fold a small piece of thick paper in half. Draw half a star against the fold, then cut it out. Open out the stencil.

Print about 20 stars.

7. Lay the stencil on a large piece of tissue paper. Dip a sponge into thick paint and dab it all over the stencil. Then, print lots more stars.

To decorate your hat like this one, use two stencils and two shades of paint.

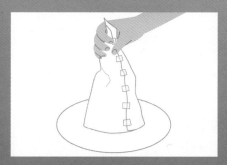

8. While the paint dries, gently squash the cone of the hat with your hands to make it crooked. Bend the brim a little, too.

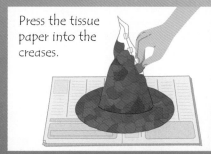

Press the tissue paper into the creases.

9. Rip lots of pieces from plain tissue paper. Brush white glue onto the hat, then press pieces of tissue paper all over it.

Try not to glue the stars over each other.

10. When the stars are dry, carefully rip around them. Glue them all over the hat, then leave the glue to dry completely.

Wizard's workshop

Draw the book and inkpot near one end of the workbench.

Don't draw his hands yet.

1. Draw a long workbench at the bottom of a large piece of paper. Then, add a book of spells and an inkpot and quill pen.

2. Draw a wizard's hat a little way above the book. Add his head and beard, then draw his face. Then, draw his body and arms.

3. Add the wizard's hands, leaving a gap between his thumb and fingers on one hand. Then, add a potion bottle, like this.

Look at this picture for ideas of what you might find in a wizard's workshop.

Fill the flasks and jars with potions, leaves and eyeballs.

Draw criss-crossed lines for the shading.

4. Draw a flask below the bottle. Add some jars and more flasks on the workbench. Then, draw a cat at one end.

5. Draw shelves above the workbench, with lots of bottles and jars on them. Then, add clouds of steam and curling lines for fumes.

6. Using watery paints, fill in the picture. Then, when the paint is dry, draw over the lines with felt-tip pens. Add some shading, too.

Add stars around the steam and fumes.

Spooky castle card

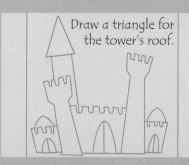
Draw a triangle for the tower's roof.

1. Fold a rectangle of thin cardboard in half, with its short ends together. Then, lay it on a piece of thick paper and draw around it.

2. Lift off the folded paper. Then, draw two crooked castle towers near the bottom of the rectangle you have drawn.

3. Draw a big entrance between the towers and a smaller one on each side of them. Add a tower to one side of the entrance, too.

4. Draw a wall above the big entrance. Add roofs and turrets on top. Then, draw another tower to the side of the castle.

Draw a thick black border, like this.

5. Draw windows and roof tiles. Then, fill in around the castle with a black felt-tip pen. Fill in any spaces between the towers, too.

You could press on a moon sticker from the sticker pages, too.

Try gluing a path,
a tree or bushes
onto your card.

Use the
silver pen.

6. Using a silver pen, carefully draw over all the pencil lines. Then, cut around the edge of the black border, like this.

7. With the fold at the top, draw a line near the top of the folded paper. Fill in the rectangle above the line with the black pen.

8. Glue the bottom of the castle onto the black rectangle. Then, draw lots of ovals for a pebbly path below the castle.

Magic spell chain

Draw two dots for the nostrils.

1. Draw a round cauldron on a large piece of thick white paper. Add two feet at the bottom and steam coming from the top.

2. Draw a spell book a little way from the cauldron. Then, draw the body and legs of a leaping frog. Add two round eyes and a face.

Paint spots on the frog, too.

3. Draw a glass bottle of magic potion with a cork in the top. Then, draw a circle for a bat's head. Add its wings, ears and face.

4. Using a thin paintbrush, fill in the pictures with paints. When they are dry, paint details such as pages in the book and bubbles.

5. Leave the paint to dry completely. Then, carefully go over all the pencil lines with a thin black felt-tip pen, like this.

6. Using the tip of a thin paintbrush, brush lines and spots of white glue on the pictures. Then, sprinkle the wet glue with glitter.

Use the ideas in these chains to make your own spell chain.

You can add any number of pictures to a spell chain.

Tape the thread to the back of the pictures.

7. When the glue is dry, gently shake off any excess glitter. Then, cut out all the pictures, leaving a white border around them.

8. To make the chain, tape the pictures onto a long piece of thread. Tape the cauldron at the bottom and the other pictures above it.

Wizard store

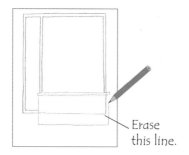

1. Draw a shape for the shelving on a piece of white paper. Add a shop counter overlapping the shelving, like this.

2. Draw a wizard's hat above the counter. Add his face and beard, then draw his body. Draw piles of coins in front of him, too.

3. Draw a ladder at one end of the counter. Add a book of spells on a book rest, next to the wizard. Draw a cash register, too.

4. Draw several shelves on the shelving behind the wizard. Then, draw a display window on the front of the counter.

5. Draw a clothes stand next to the counter. Then, add a wizard's cat and lots of cauldrons in front of the counter.

6. Add a 'Wizard Supplies Ltd.' sign above the cat. Then, draw cushions in the glass display, with magic wands and quills on them.

7. Draw lots of wizard supplies on the shelves, looking at the big picture opposite for ideas. Then, add some mice and spiders.

8. Using a thin paintbrush, carefully fill in the wizard with runny paints. Then, paint the rest of the picture and leave the paint to dry.

9. Draw over all the pencil lines with a thin black felt-tip pen. Then, write names on the labels on the jars and boxes, too.

Finger painted wizard

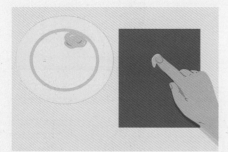

1. Mix some thick paints on a plate to make a shade for the wizard's skin. Then, finger paint his face on a piece of blue paper.

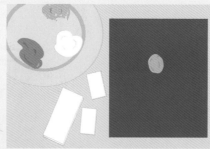

2. Pour some blue and white paint onto the plate. Then, cut one long rectangle and two shorter ones from thick cardboard.

Keep the top end in the same place.

3. Dip the edge of a short rectangle into the blue paint. Place it on the paper above the face, then scrape it around to make a hat.

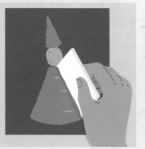

Scrape the rectangle around the bottom of the face.

4. Use the long rectangle to print a body. Then, print two arms with the short rectangle that you used to print the hat.

5. Dip the edge of the short rectangle into the paint again. Then, use it to print a straight line across the bottom of the hat.

6. Finger paint the hands, then add white hair and two pink cheeks. Then, use the second short rectangle to print a line for the wand.

Use a sticker from the sticker pages.

7. When the paint is dry, use a thin black felt-tip pen to draw the wizard's face. Press a silver star sticker onto the end of the wand.

Cut around a wizard to make a magical gift tag.

Name card

1. Finger paint a wizard's face on a piece of blue paper. Add his hat, cheeks and hair, too. Leave it to dry, then draw a face.

2. Cut around the wizard. Fold a square of thick paper in half for the card. Glue the wizard onto the card, then write the name.

You could glue wizards onto cards, writing paper and envelopes, too.

Please come to my magical wizard party at 3:00 on Saturday.
Hats and capes must be worn!

Zac

Abigail

Waldo the Wizard
Spellbound Castle
The Enchanted City

Warty toads

Draw toads sitting or jumping in different positions.

Start drawing near the top of the paper.

1. Using a pencil, draw a toad's head, with two bumps at the top. Add two round eyes in the bumps, and a wide smile.

2. Draw two front legs, with rounded toes. Add a curved line for the toad's tummy. Then, draw the two back legs, like this.

You could paint orange toads, too.

3. Using a white wax crayon, draw lots of warts on the toad's body. They are shown here in yellow so that you can see them.

The wax crayon will resist the paint.

4. Fill in the toad with watery yellow and green paints. Then, when the paint is dry, draw over the outlines again with a pencil.

You could draw a toad trying to catch a fly with its curling tongue.

Photographic manipulation: Nick Wakeford
This edition first published in 2012 by Usborne Publishing Ltd., Usborne House, 83-85 Saffron Hill, London, England. www.usborne.com
Copyright © 2012, 2006 Usborne Publishing Ltd. The name Usborne and the devices ♀♔ are Trade Marks of Usborne Publishing Ltd. All rights reserved.
No part of this publication may be reproduced, stored in a retrieval system, or transmitted in any form or by any means, electronic, mechanical, photocopying, recording or otherwise without the prior permission of the publisher. UE. This edition first published in America in 2012. Printed in Malaysia.